JUST FOR TODAY'S

homeschooling

MOM

a whisper of
ENCOURAGAMENT
when you need it most

MICHELLE HUDDLESTON

Unless otherwise indicated, all Scripture is taken from The Scriptures version. Copyright © 2014 by Institute for Scripture Research. Used by permission. All rights reserved.

All stories, advice, and encouragement related in this book are true, and used with permission by the people mentioned.

Cover design: MartinPublishingServices.com

JUST FOR TODAY'S HOMESCHOOLING MOM
Copyright © 2017 by Michelle Huddleston

ISBN-13: 978-1545028674
ISBN-10: 1545028672
Genre: Inspirational/Motivational (Self-help)

All rights reserved. No part of this publication may be reproduced, stored in a retrieval system, or transmitted in any form or by any means – electronic, mechanical, digital, photocopy, recording, or any other – except for brief quotations in printed reviews, without the prior permission of the Author.

Printed in the United States of America

Here's to You

Alex, Sapphira, Euphrates, and little one on the way... you amazing kiddos continue to teach me so much more than I feel like I could ever teach you. For that, I am forever grateful. My prayer is that through it all, you will have at least learned how to hold on to Yahweh's unchanging hand. I know there are days I've failed you as a mom, and as a teacher; however, hopefully those days are shadowed by the amazing days we have together.

Bryan, my amazing husband... I am forever grateful for your love, strength, endurance, and support that you give (and show) to me and our children. You are a true example of how to overcome anything that is thrown at you (and us). You also play a major role in homeschooling our children, something I do not ever want to take for granted.

To the mamas who read this book... may you be inspired, motivated, and encouraged in your unique journey. You are answering an incredible call in life, and it is not always easy – but oh so worth it. Cherish the good moments, learn from the not-so-good moments, and keep putting one foot in front of the other. You got this.

Your gourmet meal awaits...

The appetizer:

What you should know before the full course meal — 9

The meat:

98% mom – 2% teacher — 17

Your worst enemy — 31

The hard days — 45

The fix-all mentality — 59

The "h" word — 71

Staying true to your beliefs — 87

The sides:

There's a style for that — 101

The multiple struggle — 115

Paging Mrs. Secretary — 129

Forget the first day — 147

The dessert:

Homeschool toolbox (resources) — 161

Contact the author — 169

The appetizer.

Welcome to the appetizer portion of your gourmet meal. This dish is small, but packs a punch. You'll be glad you started with it first. This is only the beginning, so loosen your britches and get ready for one of the best meals of your life!

✱

What you should know before the full course meal

      This probably goes without saying, but I bet you are wondering what this chapter is about, and why it's referencing food. Well, it's my form of an introduction, and I just so happen to like food… a lot. And in all honesty, people rarely read introductions so I wanted to make it eye-catching and interesting.

      Now that I have your attention, when we embark on the journey of homeschooling, we have a certain picture of what homeschooling should like. Right? And when it doesn't measure up to what we dreamed, we automatically assume we're failing, or that it's not for us. If you don't struggle with that, then you must have it all mastered and don't have to read any further.

You see, this book is for the mom who doesn't have it all together. This is for the mom who sees the bigger picture, but somehow still lets self-sabotaging thoughts creep in and whisper lies. It's for the mom who hasn't quite figured out how to keep the "no soliciting" sign up to the limiting beliefs attempting to rent space in her head. This book is especially for the mom on the verge of giving up.

Do you fall in, or around, any of these categories? Then keep reading, because this is for you (and me). Whether you are a veteran homeschool mom, a brand new homeschool mom, or haven't even started yet, this book is packed with valuable information aimed to bless your socks off. I want you to know how beautiful, amazing, and extraordinary you are. The fact that you are the nurturer, chef, chauffer, master planner, calendar maker, owie-soother, *and* a teacher makes you a unique kind of superwoman.

Throughout our time together, we are going to get down to the nitty gritty. We will talk about some hot topics, and address some stuff that most don't want to tackle. The fact of the matter is, we all have emotional hard drives. Within these compartments are emotions, whether good or bad, waiting to validate whatever thoughts come into our minds. This is where limiting beliefs come into play. These are the beliefs that hinder us in some way because by believing them, our actions begin to align with them. This then causes us to have skewed views about ourselves and our self-identities.

Life and business strategist, Gary Coxe, taught me that until I understand my emotional hard drive and the limiting beliefs I have scrolling on replay, I will stay stuck in whatever thought pattern I allow my mind to process. That can seem like a tough pill to swallow, especially if you have never heard of such terminology or even know how to start the reboot process. That is another benefit of this book. We are going to do some rebooting... *together*.

There are benefits to doing occasional clean sweeps to the emotional hard drive and embracing limiting beliefs throughout the process. If we allow it, understanding self-sabotaging thoughts can reveal things about ourselves we may have been hiding, denying, and not ready to see. This process can help us get clear-headed, focused, and gain confidence in the choices we make – especially when it comes to homeschooling. There is an inner strength that can be tapped into when we face our negative emotions and limiting beliefs head on.

If you noticed the layout of the table of contents (labeled *"Your Gourmet Meal Awaits"*), you saw that this book has four sections. *The appetizer* is what you're reading now. *The meat* portion will deal with personal stuff, but still directly relates to homeschooling. *The sides* portion will dive head first into all things homeschooling, while still dealing with personal stuff. And *the desserts* part is where you'll find reliable resources and simple tools.

Each chapter in this book will uncover common concerns that come with homeschooling. You will read suggestions, recommendations, my personal struggles, comebacks, and personal advice. You will also find a few testimonies and words of encouragement from other homeschooling moms. But it won't stop there. We will also tackle some emotions and limiting beliefs that come with these concerns so we can replace them with positive ones – all which will greatly impact your overall homeschool experience (and other areas in life too).

If you have read any of my other books, then you know I am **big** on inclusion... meaning, I include everything but the kitchen sink. You'll get a dose of spirituality – particularly the belief in Yahweh (God), Yeshua Messiah (Jesus), and the Ruach HaKodesh (Holy Spirit) – scripture, prayer, and lots of space for your own note taking. I personally love when books give me space to jot down my own thoughts and revelations. So, it's only natural that I do the same when I write.

At the end of each chapter, I have included spiritual tools that highlight the following:

- limiting beliefs we as homeschool moms may face throughout our journey
- affirmations to replace those limiting beliefs (repeat these in hectic moments)
- scripture for meditation (and good for journaling)
- prayer
- journal space to notate your personal reflections

I pray you are blessed beyond measure, and that this book becomes a recurring resource for you throughout your homeschooling journey.

The meat.

Now that you've had the appetizer, are you ready to dive into the main course? Think of this portion like a huge 16oz ribeye. Not a fan of steaks? That's okay, just think of something that is super filling but still leaves room for more. We are about to dive into the heart of the matter, discussing topics and issues that lie deep beneath the surface. Grab your fork and knife and let's dive in!

✳ ✳
98% mom – 2% teacher

Let's be real. Parenting is tough. Now add being with your child 24/7 *and* being their teacher. We have just put this [sanctifying] journey on a whole new level. Funny thing is I grew up professing that I was not going to have any children. It was decided early on that I would travel the world and be all about me, me, me. Fast forward twenty years, and it's apparent God had other plans. Don't get me wrong... I'm not complaining; because looking back, I am forever grateful and incredibly blessed that He would even choose me to receive a piece of His heritage.

So, what's this percentage the title is talking about? Ninety-eight percent mom and two percent teacher is my personal logic behind being mom plus teacher, and balancing between the two. I can't say for certain that it is a concrete statistic floating around out there, but in my mind – it works.

For some reason beyond me, once we decide to homeschool, an invisible switch is flipped and suddenly, we think we must become "teacher only" during school time. Maybe you have even said, "I'm your teacher right now, not mom." Perhaps your child has had formal schooling and you have mumbled, "You wouldn't treat your teacher at school like this!" Well, of course not, because to them, you are mom! No matter how many hats we wear, we will always be mom first to our children.

I'm not sure if it is the ex-teacher in me or what, but I found myself forgetting that I need to always be mom first. Alex, our firstborn, was in the prime of his adolescence when we started homeschooling. He had spent his first two and a half years in my mother's home daycare, and his preschool and kindergarten years in public school. Off and on during those years, I worked in the school system and early childhood field as a tutor, teacher's aide, and lead preschool teacher.

Even if your background looks nothing like that, it still seems that we all must get over the same hurdle of remembering that we are mom first. And never forgetting that no matter how old our children get, they still need their mom. One homeschooling mom reminded me that our children may have adolescent chips on their shoulder, but they need their mama before they need their teacher. This single piece of advice is what makes the relationships we have with our children more important, and why they should come first... even before homeschooling.

If you had formal schooling as a child, think back to those few teachers who still hold a special place in your heart. Why is that? Is it because they exhibited motherly characteristics? Were they nurturing in a sense that helped you trust them? Did they see themselves beyond the teacher role? My first-grade teacher, Mrs. Stooksbury, was like that. She was much more than a teacher. You could tell that she cared about each one of her students. To her, we were more than students. She saw us as her children. The passion that poured from her is one that still impacts me right now today.

When you ask a homeschool mom why she wanted to start homeschooling, you'll often hear an answer that sounds a lot like what Mrs. Stooksbury offered. *I want to be the primary nurturer and/or dominant teacher in my child's life.* Or, *I want to be sure my children get a great start in life.* These responses, and many others, come from a place of love and nurture that occur naturally within the journey of motherhood.

Our older kids are kids who still need their mama.
Melinda G. – Philadelphia, PA

Let's switch gears for a moment and think about another awesome opportunity that comes with being ninety-eight percent mom and two percent teacher. Most of the time, when we are looking through the mom lens, I believe we have better discernment when issues arise. We will be able to clearly see that every issue may not be a homeschooling issue. There are times when it may be a parenting matter or a concern with the child. In the beginning, it may be difficult to determine the underlying factor. Nevertheless, with time, patience, and wisdom it becomes easier to figure out.

For example, there may be days when you just really don't want to *do school.* For whatever reason is beside the point. Yet, what also runs parallel is how our children can pick up on what kind of day we are having. Suppose they also take on the emotions and feelings of not really wanting to school that day. So, it comes out in what seems like Suzy regressing because she is taking extra-long to complete one worksheet (whereas yesterday she was done in five minutes).

Often, instead of remembering that we may very well be the underlying issue... it is covered by placing the attention on Suzy taking too long. Hence, making it an issue with the child. This can fuel the frustration that was already brewing. Causing tension, which can lead to a small lash out towards Suzy not being up to par that day, and so on. In all actuality, if we take a step back and adjust the mommy lens, the whole ordeal could fall under a parenting matter versus a homeschool matter.

Of course, these things will happen. We will overlook some details. And we may not always get it right. But at least we know that at the end of the day, we are mom, and God has equipped us to do this. Not only does being ninety-eight percent mom and two percent teacher reward us with being able to stay mom and help discern between issues, but, we are also able to work on establishing and maintaining trust with our children throughout the teaching process.

You know that feeling you get when you call your best friend to vent, knowing she isn't going to run and tell everyone else? Or the comfort in knowing that you can confide in your spouse, and he will still love you no matter what? Imagine how our children feel when they know they can open their hearts to us… especially about homeschooling concerns.

    I don't know how it is in your home, but I like to include Alex in what I'm deciding to do for his schooling. Maybe not for *everything*, but there are times where I want his input. I want him to know that I care about what he thinks. Not only does it give him the ability to have a voice, but it also builds trust in our ever-growing relationship as mother and son. He may not realize it, but this simple tactic trickles over into other areas.

    An incident happened a little over a year ago where Alex had broken a toy while playing. He didn't tell me (or his father) until I came across the broken toy while cleaning. I asked why he didn't tell me about it, and replied, "Because I was scared that you would be upset and I would get in trouble." I used that as an opportunity to tell him about the importance of letting me or his dad know when he breaks something. I specifically explained the type of consequence that would come with the conduct exhibited so he would not have to second-guess coming forth, should something similar arise in the future.

    Almost a year later, he broke one of my nice, thick, pastel brown, glass pots (that I used for almost everything that needed boiling) and he immediately came and told me. Not only did he tell me right after it happened, but he also said it with confidence, knowing that he wasn't going to get in major trouble. We cleaned it up together, and I was able to teach him how to properly clean up glass. I would like to thank the many times that I've been able to continuously build trust between us so that he grows up knowing that he can tell me anything – from not understanding why he should learn division to breaking a dish!

I hope you see that being mom is the greatest, most rewarding role we could ever have. And being a homeschooling mom just adds to that reward. It's not easy. There are some hurdles to jump and hills to climb. We may even have thoughts that make us second-guess if motherhood is really our calling. Couple that with a rollercoaster of emotions and we might even begin to think just maybe homeschooling wasn't such a good idea. But in the greater scheme of things, this gives us purpose. It gives us the opportunity to pour back into the Kingdom by raising and equipping spiritually strong children.

This legacy goes far beyond the hard days, the second-thoughts, and mind struggles. It will reach into generations and equip our sons and daughters to be who God intended them to be. Without apology. I'll warn you now about the next few chapters. We are going to dig deep and talk about some tough stuff that comes along with this journey. If you are a new homeschooling mom, it's not to scare you. It's to prepare you, and help establish you.

In the spiritual toolbox on the next page, we will look at some limiting beliefs that come with being ninety-eight percent mom and two percent teacher. There are some affirmations to trump those beliefs, along with scripture, prayer, and journal space to help get you through some trying times.

You're the mom, and God has equipped you to do this.
Gina G. - LaGrange, KY

Spiritual Tools

Oh, sweet sister. How amazing was our time today? Pardon me for shedding a few tears, but I couldn't help myself. Being mom before anything else isn't always easy. It seems to become just another hat we wear, doesn't it? As you read the next several pages, be encouraged in knowing this is only the beginning. We are both growing, no matter where we are in our journey's, and I'm excited to grow with you!

Be transformed by the renewing of your mind!

Limiting beliefs:

- I'm not a good mom.
- I'm afraid I'm not doing a good job.
- My children deserve a better mom.
- That mom is so much better than me.
- I don't know how to be mom and teacher.
- I can't gain the trust of my children.

Affirmations:

- I am the best mom I know how to be.
- God has blessed my children with me as their mom.
- I will not compare myself to other moms.
- I will be mom first, and teacher second.
- I am gaining the trust of my children with each opportunity we are given.

Scripture for Meditation

Jeremiah 29:11 – 'For I know the plans I am planning for you,' declares Yahweh, 'plans of peace and not of evil, to give you a future and an expectancy.'

Psalm 127:3 – Look, children are an inheritance from Yahweh, the fruit of the womb is the reward.

Proverbs 22:6 – Train up a child in the way he should go, even when he is old he turns not away from it.

Ephesians 6:4 – And you, fathers, do not provoke your children, but bring them up in the instruction and admonition of the Master.

Colossians 3:23-24 – And whatever you do, do it heartily, as to the Master and not to men, knowing that from the Master you shall receive the reward of the inheritance. It is the Master, Messiah, you serve.

Let us pray,

Merciful Father, You are so gracious. It is such a privilege to be chosen as a carrier of Your heritage. Thank You for the ability, the willingness, and the desire to be a mother, and a teacher. Your plans of peace give us an expectancy of the future. Abba, we commit all our doings to you, knowing that our reward comes from You, and not from men.

We seek to satisfy You, and always keep your will and ways first and foremost in all we say and do. May we never lose focus of what is most important. We pray that our children will be receptive throughout our homeschool journey's. We pray that we will keep the balance between being mom and teacher.

Cover our families with the wing of your protection. In the name of Yeshua our Messiah, amen.

Personal Reflections

* * *

Your worst enemy

You know the old saying, "Sticks and stones may break my bones, but words will never hurt me."? Yeah, well, I'm calling all kinds of bluff on that one. My curiosity went through the roof when thinking about this little saying, and I had to know its origin. Apparently, it dates to March 1862, where it was reported to have first been mentioned in a publication of the African Methodist Episcopal Church. (Whoa!)

If that wasn't enough, in 1972 it appeared as advice in *Tappy's Chicks: and Other Links between Nature and Human Nature* (by Mrs. George Cupples). And it wouldn't be fair if it didn't end up in a song. So, to keep it going, The Who's featured it in their 1981 song, The Quiet One. In the most recent days, it is simply known as an English language children's rhyme. A rhyme meant to persuade children that name-calling, belittling, and any other forms of verbal bullying doesn't have to be harmful. Again, I'm calling major bluff! (By the way, teach those tidbits of info to your kids and you've just completed a history lesson. You're welcome.)

The fact of the matter is, words **do** hurt. Especially when they are coming from within. When words have become thoughts that attach themselves to all sorts of emotions, it can be painful. When disregarded, emotions ranging from doubt to regret can kindle what could end up being a huge forest fire.

I surely don't believe that we allow these negative emotions and thoughts run amuck in our minds on purpose. What I *do* believe is that it is normal to deal with them. Where the problem lies, though, is *how* they are being dealt with.

It usually takes something to trigger the negative emotion/thought before we realize that it is even there. For example, when my husband and I decided that we were going to homeschool, I began telling my closest family and friends about it. As in most cases, majority of who we told were not understanding of our decision. In their misunderstandings, words were spoken that attached on to my emotions and thoughts of fear that would occasionally spin out of control and cause me to second-guess what we decided.

I began questioning myself, asking things like, *"Can I really do this? Where do I even start? Will my children learn all they are supposed to know? Who will be watching us? What will I teach? Do I remember how to-?"* You see where I'm going with this? Not saying that it comes easy to nip in the bud early, but over time (and with lots of practice), it can be.

Let's talk about the preconceived notion that "homeschooling moms should be happy, perfect, and have it all together." Feel free to belly laugh, because I sure did when I had that thought! Where does this even come from? Oh, I know. It comes from the place of comparison. The place where you begin searching the internet for things you can implement into your homeschool... and for some reason, almost every picture is of a happy-go-lucky, I-do-everything-right mom followed by the best-looking kids. You know what I'm talking about.

This can be even worse if you are part of a local homeschool co-op group. When you get a bunch of homeschool moms together, it can genuinely be a great time. Until you get away from it all and start remembering how well-behaved Sally's kids were. Or how Marie talked about having her entire year planned by July. And how LeeAnne seemed so confident in the curriculum you once tried that resulted in more tears and hair loss than a single completed lesson.

Can we say comparison overdrive? Um, yeah! But... good thing is, it happens to all of us at some point:

When I first began homeschooling, I was intimidated by other mothers. I felt like I was inferior and not up for the task. A fellow homeschooler pulled me aside and said, "when you compare, you lose. Your children lose. You know your children best. Teach from a place of love."
Angela H. - Cincinnati, OH

What often goes [un]talked about is what lies at the root of this comparison game. This is where it can look slightly different for each person. For me, it is usually fear of not measuring up. Not measuring up to what exactly? Truth be told, it is my own expectations. Of course, I could place some of the blame on wanting to measure up to what I believe others are doing, or what the State says I should be doing – but really, it all derives from expectations I have put on myself.

We can't forget that there are outside forces at work, but that's where we learn to build a barrier of resistance. Not in a negative way; but, in a way that protects our mind, heart, and emotions. The outside forces, or external expectations placed on you by others, must be addressed too, because they **will** happen. I remember first voicing our concrete decision to homeschool, and boy oh boy did people come out of the woodworks to give their opinion about it.

"Why do you want to do that? Aren't you worried about socialization? How do you know what to teach? Are you sure you're qualified enough to educate them? You know the State will be watching you! How long are you going to do it? What do homeschoolers do? Will they ever get to go on field trips?" And on and on the questions rolled in. I thought to myself, *"WOW!"* Some of them I couldn't answer right off the bat because I simply didn't know the answer. Some questions had me questioning my abilities to homeschool. And some questions sparked me to really take a deeper look at the benefits of homeschooling.

What I didn't have, in the beginning, was that barrier of resistance I talked about a little bit ago. I was concrete in my choice to homeschool, but that's as far as that went. I didn't know how to protect my mind, heart, and emotions from what would arise once our news went public. I now understand it deals with my own emotional hard drive, my own internal struggles, and how to process out what didn't need to "rent space in my head" (as Gary Coxe would say).

While people may not realize that their questions, comments, criticisms, and concerns often show their lack of support and understanding – it still isn't their fault how we perceive what they say. We have the control of how we let it affect us. Yes, we have decided to put our children's education in our hands, and regardless of what it looks like, that is okay!

What about our internal struggles? Oh, goodness. Are you thinking, *"Where do I even start with that?"* Yeah, me too. Let's start here: **we have a lot on our plates**. Some moms are working homeschool moms. Other moms are stay-at-home, homeschooling four, five, six+ children. Wherever you are on that scale, we can all agree that we have a lot on our plates. Behind the planning, organizing, arranging, ordering, typing, printing, and budgeting is a mom who fights stressing, worrying, competing, comparing, doubting, and trusting. It's totally natural.

So, who is our worst enemy? Family and friends who show lack of support until years down the road once they see we are all making it alive? The public/private school mentality of people who make it a point to question us in a degrading way? The other homeschool moms who always have it all together, or so we think? Or is it ourselves, with our own emotions and personal internal struggles?

BINGO! It's us, y'all! It is absolutely necessary to take ownership of our part in our struggles, and this can be a comforting realization. This awareness unlocks the ability to take control when our worst enemy spikes her ugly head. As Scripture reminds us – we can take every thought captive. Especially those that raise themselves against the knowledge of our Messiah. It doesn't mean that we won't ever have thoughts that test our resolve. Quite the opposite. We **will** have thoughts that will force us to go against every emotion and every internal struggle so that we can continue to walk confidently in what God has called us to do.

When we fail to recognize the moments we are being our own worst enemy, it adds up. Over time, it usually results in something happening that takes a similar form of "blowing a gasket." This becomes the perfect time to take a step back to redirect. First, we should realize that maybe we missed the boat dock and need turn this ship around to try again. Next, reflect to see what can be done differently. Lastly, address how we can react in a way that strengthens our barrier of resistance. And just like learning to ride a bike, we'll get good at it. We'll confidently have answers to those questions that once made us feel insecure or uncomfortable. And we will be able to help guide a new homeschooling mom through the stressors of her first year.

If we want to be totally honest, spending too much time on our insecurities, failures, and faults is selfish. We can't be much help to our children, our families, and others when we are so focused on ourselves. I'm not saying to not spend time working on you (I know you understand what I mean). I'm just bringing perspective to the fact that we don't have to give our worst enemy more time than she needs to live, learn, and grow.

So, when she comes, learn what you must learn. Put on the shelf what needs to be put on the shelf (for later). And keep it moving. Don't make a habit of dwelling too much on those negative thoughts, emotions, external expectations, and internal struggles. Just keep moving forward.

Spiritual Tools

Alright, sister. Have you made your list of things to get? No soliciting signs. Check. No vacancies sign. Check. I'd say we are off to a great start. As you read the next several pages, focus on replacing the negative thoughts with positive ones. Repeat positive affirmations, write them down several times, put them on notecards and place them around your home. Your mind will thank you for it.

Be transformed by the renewing of your mind!

Limiting beliefs:

- I'm worried about what others think.
- I feel guilty for pulling my kids out of school.
- My schooling doesn't look like [hers].
- That mom knows so much.
- I don't think I am enough.
- I am always stressed about this.

Affirmations:

- I will seek what God says about me.
- I am making the best decision for my children.
- I know my children best.
- I am more than a conqueror.
- I choose to let go of what I do not understand.

Scripture for Meditation

Isaiah 26:3 – "The one steadfast of mind You guard in perfect peace, for he trusts in You."

Zephaniah 3:17 – "Yahweh your Elohim in your midst, is mighty to save. He rejoices over you with joy, He is silent in His love, He rejoices over you with singing."

Psalm 16:11 – You show me the path of life; in Your presence is joy to satisfaction; at Your right hand are pleasures forever.

Psalm 29:11 – Yahweh gives strength to His people; Yahweh blesses His people with peace.

Proverbs 3:5-6 – Trust in Yahweh with all your heart, and lean not on your own understanding. Know Him in all your ways, and He makes all your paths straight.

Let us pray,

Gracious Father. Good, good Father. It is truly who You are. You know our lying down, and our rising up. You awesomely and wonderfully made us. And for that we are forever grateful. We want to be steadfast of mind and trust in You because you will guard us in perfect peace.

In moments that we are not thinking straight, we ask that you renew our minds and create in us a steadfast spirit. Bring to our remembrance what You say about us and not what we hear from ourselves and others.

In our time of weakness, increase our strength. Form a barrier of protection around our emotions, thoughts, and actions. Deal with any negative emotions we have stored up that are preventing us from walking in the fullness of your joy.

Cover our family's mind and thoughts with the wing of your protection. In the name of Yeshua our Messiah, amen.

Personal Reflections

****

The hard days

There. Will. Be. Hard. Days. Possibly hard years, for that matter. Period. Exclamation point! If a homeschool mom tells you that she doesn't have hard days, smile and walk away. Seriously, it would be bizarre to think otherwise. Nonetheless, hard days/years do not get the final say unless you allow them. They are not the deciding factor that determine whether you are successful or not, unless you give in to that stinkin' thinkin' we talked about last chapter. And keep in mind that all teachers (and parents) have hard days and rocky years. It doesn't matter if you are homeschooling, public schooling, or private schooling. It's the same across the board.

What does a hard day look like? I would have to say it depends on the person, the child, the family, and the day overall. I've had a great day go down the drain fast because of a little printer problem. It was supposed to be a productive day. It started out smoothly enough. I'd survived breakfast, done some easy morning work and I was feeling pretty proud about the great deal of effort I put into preparing the day's lessons.

As I normally would, I went to print those wonderful pages I'd worked so hard on and my printer randomly decided it was going on vacation never to return. It messed me up because it messed up my flow. I just so happen to not have anything else in mind to do and because of the time it took to try and fix the printer, I was over it. Over the lesson. Over the school day. Just over it.

Looking back, it's comical. Especially when paired to an actual hard day that looks like two sick babies and an older child who strategically forgets a concept that was just taught the week before. And because of his "forgetfulness," it was making the current assignment nearly impossible without re-teaching last week's lesson. Did I mention the two sick babies? Oh yeah, the constant holding, pampering, changing of diapers and clothes – all while trying to backtrack.

Some hard days end in a coloring sheet, an educational movie, along with both mom and kids shedding a few tears. Even then, it is still worth it. There is something about overcoming hard days and persevering that is super rewarding. Not to mention, some of the most amazing lessons are learned on the toughest days.

I started out traditional teaching. We were both frustrated and crying by the third month.
Shateeka O. - Hopkinsville, KY

We have established that hard days can look like a broken printer, forgetful kiddos, and shed tears. Hard years can take much of the same covering, but it just seems like an eternity. Still, a hard year doesn't mean give up. There are ways to make these hard times work for our benefit.

One way is to reflect and think about how often the hard days are happening. Are they sporadic? Is there a pattern? Are days going well until a certain subject is taught? Is there any resistance toward a particular teaching style? Don't worry, we will talk about teaching styles in a later chapter. In the meantime, while there are many more questions that could be asked, these are just a few to consider.

For now, let's pretend that we have pinpointed the issue to be resistance toward a certain subject. Knowing this, we can look for ways to change up the way the subject is presented, taught, and learned. This can be in the form of less worksheets, and more interactive activities. More video/movie lessons and less reading. In some cases, a verbal report is easier than a handwritten one. While these are just suggestive examples, and not a fix all, the idea I hope you are gathering here is that sometimes a small adjustment can relieve a hard day. And there are days when we all need some relief.

In the beginning, I noticed my hard days came when I tried to do things the way I remember them being done in public school. The *sitting at the desk while the teacher stands at the board* approach would only work for a little while. If I took too long, I could tell by Alex's body language. He would start playing with his pencil, then nibbling on the eraser, taking extra-long to write down the board notes, and so on. Before realizing that I needed to switch things up a bit, I would see *him* as the issue and try to force *him* to accommodate to how I wanted to teach. Sound familiar?

Another way to make a hard day work in your favor is to use it as a time to take a small break. If the day is starting to go south early, improvise and go south with it. What I mean is close the books, put down the pencils, and do something completely different. Take a family walk around the neighborhood. Go to the local park. Have a picnic in the back yard. Just do something different, and refreshing.

Sometimes hard days are indicators that we need to relax. Do you remember your first year where everything needed to go by the schedule you made? The children needed to be comfortable in the schoolroom you created. And the curriculum you purchased was the next best thing to sliced bread. All this preparation was supposed to work in your favor, without fail. Then, the hard days came and it all seemed to fall apart just as fast as you put it together. Looking back on it, it would have been much easier to embrace the switch-up, or the relax and refresh techniques, eh? We know now that this is totally okay, and acceptable!

A few moms I know use the journal technique on their hard days. They improvise the lessons for that day and take moments to reflect in the form of writing. Journaling offers what I call R&R, and I'm not talking about rest and relaxation. It provides a way to *reflect* in written detail and the ability to *revisit* a past account without having to flip through the mind's rolodex of memories. This can make analyzing hard days a lot easier.

In keeping with the theme of relaxation, I'm excited to share a few techniques I have learned that help me to release everyday stress and anxiety. When a day becomes stressful, I like to get in a quiet place and pray. When I want (or need) to involve my kiddos, we will play relaxing music and lay on the floor in our own spots. I ask them to close their eyes and listen to the different sounds. This gives me another moment to relax, and pray.

When things get rough, take a step back and think on all the good things. The way your kid makes you laugh or a good deed they have done or just how unique they are... and count it all JOY!!
Shateeka O. - Hopkinsville, KY

I couldn't have said it better myself. Counting every hard day, and every hard year, as joy is a sure way to find the fuel to keep moving forward. Accepting that there **will** be hard days is the single best thing we can do for ourselves, our children, and families. Acceptance opens the door to embracing any changes that need to be made, and strength to follow through without the guilt and self-doubt. Simply put, hard days are part of the journey. And, despite the hardships, the journey remains worthwhile.

Spiritual Tools

Are you looking forward to the hard days? I am! And I hope you are too, sister! Why, you ask? Because, remember... hard days teach us lessons. And while they are not fun while we are going through them, it is sure to lead us to growth on the other side. As read the next several pages, I hope you are inspired to have a different outlook on the hard days. In the end, they are not always as bad as they seem.

Be transformed by the renewing of your mind!

Limiting beliefs:

- I don't know how to handle hard days.
- I don't know what I am doing wrong.
- Hard days must mean this isn't for us.
- Maybe my children need different schooling.
- Everything I try doesn't make it better.
- I'm losing faith in my ability to homeschool.

Affirmations:

- I will find ways to improvise on hard days.
- I have the ability to change how hard days make me feel.
- Our good days outweigh the hard days.
- I am fit to homeschool my children with grace.
- God is my strength in the midst of weakness.

Scripture for Meditation

Isaiah 40:31 - But those who wait on Yahweh renew their strength, they raise up the wing like eagles, they run and are not weary, they walk and do not faint.

Psalm 55:2 - Give heed to me, and answer me, I wander and moan in my complaint.

Proverbs 16:20 - He who acts wisely concerning the Word finds good, and blessed is he who trusts in Yahweh.

Galatians 6:9 - And let us not lost heart in doing good, for in due season we shall reap if we do not grow weary.

Philippians 4:13 - I have strength to do all, through Messiah who empowers me.

James 1:19 - So then, my beloved brothers, let every man be swift to hear, slow to speak, slow to wrath.

Let us pray,

Wonderful Father. Your Word is a lamp to our feet and a light to our path. We are thankful that when we have hard days, we can find comfort in knowing that You are there in the midst. We can remember that our strength is renewed in You.

Although we complain, we pray that you would hear our voice and answer us. We will not lose heart in doing good, especially on hard days, because Your Word says that we will reap if we do not grow weary. Especially on hard days, we will seek to be slow to anger, yet be mindful of what we hear and speak.

Thank You in advance for difficult days because they teach us to increase our faith and belief. We know they will work out for our good and for Your glory.

Cover our families with the wing of your protection. In the name of Yeshua our Messiah, amen.

Personal Reflections

✽ ✽ ✽ ✽ ✽
The fix-all mentality

In homeschool dreamland, there is a fix-all mentality. Sort of like a one-size fits all. It's thinking you can snap a finger, and everything will be perfect. It's believing the schedule you set back in June will work to a T when August arrives... or throughout the entire school year without fail. It's thinking the first curriculum you choose is going to be the one that works for each child (and forever). How easily do we get caught in this type of thinking? Probably more often than we would like to admit. If we are honest with ourselves, is that what we really want though?

I think most of us would agree that a perfect day involves not having to scrub crayon off the wall or bargain with the 5th grader to get him to complete the day's lessons. A good schedule involves getting a few assignments done in a timely manner, and a sign of a great curriculum is simply seeing our children smile after completing an assignment. On the other hand, maybe a perfect day involves getting the laundry done, a decent meal cooked, and next week's plans written on the calendar. That's a huge accomplishment in my home!

Nevertheless, in replacement of the fix-all mentality, I'd like to suggest an alternative perspective to consider. I like using word pictures and illustrations, so imagine with me, if you will, that successful homeschooling is a lot like working through a maze that includes all kinds of doors. Some doors open to immovable walls and dead ends. They are the doors of lack of vision, lack of confidence, mom guilt, etc. They look good, and seem right, but lead you into struggle and hardship.

On the other hand, there are other doors that open to freedom, refuge, protection, and confidence. They lead you to homeschooling success. Now imagine yourself holding a key ring with every key you'll ever need to unlock your success. The key you will use most often is labeled with just one word, and while it is small in spelling, it seems mighty to achieve. I could end the book right here with this concept, but we have a lot more to talk about.

Are you ready? Here it goes...

T-R-U-S-T

  Yep, that's it! Trust. It seems so simple, doesn't it? But think about it. If it were as simple as it sounds, then why does Scripture repeatedly remind us to trust in Yahweh? Instead of fear, trust. Trust, and you will be blessed. There is refuge in trust. There is protection in trust. Confidence is found in trust. There is freedom in trust. And so on. Truth be told, as long as we are in this life, we will encounter some sort of hardship, struggle, obstacle, problem, or whatever you want to call it. But it is never to break us – only build us. When we put our trust in Abba, even going through the doors that look like failure and dead ends ultimately lead us right into our purpose. He can use it, and always seems to make it all work for our good. Isn't that comforting? I would say so!

  Now that we have established trust as the master key that unlocks many doors, let's talk about the keys that don't quite fit. For starters, there is the key of unexpected expectations. You know, the expectancies we've placed on ourselves that are just asking for an anxiety attack. This key will only work once we begin to set realistic outlooks. When we set realistic expectations, we are subconsciously operating with trust. It won't be stressful, heartbreaking, or nerve-wrecking. It will fit like the missing piece of a puzzle.

Next, there is the key of energy. How is your energy spread? Too thin? Gone by lunchtime? I would be lying if I spoke as though I had this one figured out. But, having been pregnant every year since 2013 gives me some kind of pass, doesn't it? Maybe, but even then, *trusting* the season of our family expanding also means *trusting* that Yahweh will provide me with the strength I need.

This is where I may get a little "preachy" so stay with me. I know Yahweh will provide me with what I need to get whatever task done. Got it. I also know that I can't just sit back and twiddle my thumbs while I wait for some divine outpouring to hit my head like the water from a shower nozzle. Right? For so many years, I never really considered what *I* needed to *do* to receive what Scripture says is mine. Are you going where I'm saying?

Let's revisit the topic of energy, for example. If I'm going to continue with a routine that obviously tires me down, leaving me with nothing to give by the afternoon, should I keep this routine while helplessly quoting, "His strength will be made perfect in my weakness!"? No! Obviously, something needs to change, right? Yes! Perhaps Yahweh will strengthen my mind to come up with a new routine that doesn't leave me tired by noon. Or, perhaps He will put someone in my path who gives me an idea of something to try. No matter how it comes, I know that it will take some level of me doing something instead of sitting back waiting to be moved like a puppet.

Before wrapping up, I want to touch base with the key of mom guilt. We all struggle with this at some point. Can't go on field trips because of a work schedule? Unable to participate in co-op because of conflicting scheduling? Had to decide to use another curriculum because of financial limitations? No matter the reason for the guilt, it doesn't have to affect you or homeschool days. These may appear to make a day harder, but it doesn't have to be that way. Remind yourself of the season you are in and prioritize accordingly.

This past year, we had to sit an entire semester out of our local homeschool group. This meant missing coop, which I usually teach a class or two. We missed field trips, and I just so happened to be on the fieldtrip committee this year. Our son missed the annual spelling bee, which he won for his grade category last year. And there were several other extra-curricular activities we had to miss that had been written on the calendar since the semester before.

Did I go through mom guilt? You bet! However, what held it off from becoming ongoing attacking thoughts was being okay with having to reprioritize due to a family hardship. It had nothing to do with homeschooling, but being involved in the homeschool group had to take a back seat. And guess what, it only took about six months to recover and we will be able to dive back in this upcoming year! What seemed bad turned for good.

No matter what your case may be, I hope you understand what I am saying through all of this. Somehow, we must toss the mind-trapping thought that there is a fix-all, because there isn't. What we can rely on is the fact that if we trust Yahweh, trust ourselves, and trust the process of this journey... we will have better, and more meaningful, experiences.

Loving my daughter is not enough, choosing a good path is not enough, praying is not enough, even solely putting my trust in God is not enough... faith not only requires believing, but in many cases, it requires thoughts, vision and action.
Faith. S - New York, New York

Spiritual Tools

That one-size-fits-all mentality can sure creep up on us, can't it, sister? I am so guilty of allowing it to persuade me that I should do something because someone else is doing it. Instead, I should be more focused on doing what I'm doing because it is what **works** for me and my family. As you read the next several pages, I want you to consider areas that you've let the fix-all mentality overstep and wreak havoc in your mind. Focus on conquering that thought process, and replacing it with trust in Yahweh, and trust in yourself.

Be transformed by the renewing of your mind!

Limiting beliefs:

- If I could only get it right.
- I just need to fix _____.
- Maybe I should do what "they" are doing.
- If only I could _____.
- I don't trust myself to do a good job.
- I'm losing trust in my ability to homeschool.

Affirmations:

- I trust myself to make the right decisions.
- It is okay to not fix everything at the same time.
- I will do what is best for my family.
- I will trust Yahweh and what His Word says.
- I will trust myself and our unique homeschooling journey.

Scripture for Meditation

Deuteronomy 2:3 – 'You have gone around this mountain long enough, turn northward.'

Joshua 1:9 – "Have I not commanded you? Be strong and courageous Do not be afraid, nor be discouraged, for Yahweh your Elohim is with you wherever you go."

Psalm 13:5 – But I have trusted in Your loving-commitment; my heart rejoices in Your deliverance.

Psalm 84:12 – O Yahweh of hosts, blessed is the man who trusts in You!

Romans 15:13 – And the Elohim of expectation fill you will al joy and peace in believing, that you overflow with expectation by the power of the Set-apart Spirit.

Let us pray,

Most trustworthy Father. It is in You that we will put our trust. We will not look to the right, or to the left, but we will follow where Your voice leads. Thank You for the ability to homeschool, and may we never take it for granted.

We do not want to focus on how to make everything perfect, but to see Your love perfected in all we say and do. Lead, guide, and direct our thoughts so they are stayed on You.

Help us to see where we are missing the mark. We welcome Your correction because we know that it will help keep us on track. Search us and know our heart. Try us, and know our anxious thoughts. If there be anything in us that is a hindrance, let us see it.

Cover our families with the wing of your protection. In the name of Yeshua our Messiah, amen.

Personal Reflections

✱ ✱ ✱ ✱ ✱ ✱

The "h" word

In the beginning of the homeschooling journey, it can seem overwhelming. Okay, who am I kidding? Every homeschool mom I talk to agrees that it doesn't "seem" overwhelming. On the contrary, it *is* overwhelming. Thoughts of, *"Where do I start? What curriculum do I purchase? What's the legal process? And, will there be support?"* will cloud the mind. This can lead us to believe that it is not okay to talk about what we're dealing with. It nonchalantly gets brushed off and we begin to think, *"This is my journey and something I need to do alone."*

The fact of the matter is, it's okay to admit that we are dealing with the struggles that come with homeschooling. It is okay to admit that **we need HELP, and ask for it**. *gasp* Did I just say the "h" word? I sure did. Now say it with me: **It is okay to need and ask for HELP**. We are not alone. Never think for one moment that you should do any of this by yourself.

I want you to take a little quiz. Don't worry, your answers are for your eyes only and simply to help with self-reflection.

1. On a scale of 1-10, how comfortable are you asking for help? _____
2. If you answered 6 or below, can you identify why you aren't comfortable asking for help?
   _____
   _____
3. How important is it for you to have a support system? _____
4. Do you have a couple of trustworthy people you could ask for help? Who are they?
   _____
5. If you don't have a physical support system, where do you go for help? (Google, Facebook groups, blogs, etc.)
   _____
   _____

6. How often do you reach out for help?

_____

Put these answers to the side for now as you continue reading. My hope is by the end of this chapter you will have a different outlook (if needed) on asking for help, feeling comfortable accepting it, and having more confidence to put the help received into action.

Let's start by addressing the daunting question that everyone practically has the same answer for.

Why don't we ask for help?

The first answer I typically hear is, *"I don't want to bother anyone with my issues."* Or, *"I don't want to waste so-and-so's time."* Okay, I get it. We don't want to bother people so we would rather figure this thing out on our own, end up reinventing the wheel, and still end up needing to reach out to someone who has been there and done that. Am I right?

Let me insert a little disclaimer right quick – I apologize ahead of time because this is going to step on some toes (it did mine). The *real* root of why we don't reach out to others is because of pride. Pride takes many shapes and forms, and the trickiest characteristic it has is the ability to play on a person's fear. By the time we get through talking ourselves out of something, we don't even realize that we let pride turn into fear. Then fear turns into doubt.

It's no wonder that Scripture says we have not because we ask not. I don't want to twist it out of its contextual meaning, but the principle itself makes sense. Pride tells us not to ask for help because we may bother someone. Pride will then say that we can do it ourselves, and we do not need help. However, where is pride when we are struggling and really could use a helping hand? Oh, it's right there ready to take the shape of fear and doubt. *"Well, this is just too hard. I don't think I can do this anymore. Why don't I just ---."*

See the cycle? How many times have you been caught on that merry-go-round? I have, more times than I want to admit. My husband has helped me tremendously in getting over being too prideful to ask for help. In the beginning of our marriage, he would tell me, *"I can tell when you need help, but I'm just waiting for you to ask."* That hit me hard, but made so much sense. I realized I needed to come to the place where I could actually say it, *and accept* it.

Whoa. Here is another layer we need to peel. Acceptance. Not only should we drop our pride to ask for help, but we must drop our pride to accept help. Have you ever been in a situation where someone shared some advice, and the whole time you are thinking, *"I really don't think that's going to work for me"* or *"This sounds crazy."*? Then you realize down the road they were right. It did work. And, it was just what you needed! Can we say acceptance issue with a touch of pride? Probably.

Of course, this isn't the case with everything. There are times when we genuinely should disregard something suggested to us, especially if it comes against our morals, values, and beliefs. This is where discernment and deliberately choosing our support circle comes into play. This is also why I asked if you had a couple of trustworthy people to count on; and, how important is it for you to have a support system you could truly depend on. Beyond the pride, fear, and doubt, we need these accountability partners, so to speak. And not just for homeschooling, but for other areas of life as well.

So, what's the downfall of staying quiet when we desperately need to speak out? Added stress. Intense moments. Anxiety. Mom guilt. No matter the end, failure to not ask for help is a risk that we shouldn't be willing to take so easily. I don't know about you, but I have experienced some dark moments from being too prideful, fearful, or doubtful to ask for help. It resulted in periods of seclusion and setbacks. Times where even if I wanted to reach out, no one was there. Be thankful if you have never experienced it on that level.

Enough about the toe-stepping tango with why we don't ask for help. Let's talk about the benefits that come *with asking*. When we are comfortable asking for help, and we reach out to those we trust, it becomes a pressure reliever. Wouldn't you agree? There is something about picking up the phone, and saying, *"Hey girl. What are your thoughts and/or experiences about (insert issue)?"* Knowing that on the other end is an honest answer takes the pressure off trying to figure it all out on your own.

Less pressure is something we could definitely use as homeschooling moms. We already have the pressure of being our husband's helpmate, caring for the children, preparing and cooking meals, grocery shopping, laundry, and cleaning the home. Oh, and let's not forget the extra-curricular activities, sports, clubs, and so on. Throw in homeschooling and we have just added an entirely new pressure to our journey.

This makes having a great support system even more important. Along with less pressure comes the peace of knowing that we can trust in quality resources. When I call my friends Christina and Asian, I know their advice, suggestions, and experiences are something I do not have to second-guess. I trust they would not tell me something that is not true or would hinder me in some way.

There are also quality resources that we can trust that may not come directly from someone we know. It takes searching, sifting, and checking but they are out there. I suggest checking a resource with another friend to see if they are familiar with it. Perhaps they have used it, or are willing to take a look at it. I go this far because as I mentioned before, we must protect our emotions, minds, and hearts.

Another benefit to having a good support system, and being willing to ask for (and accept) help is the humbling experience. I believe it speaks so much of a person when they can admit they need help. Something special happens when a person becomes transparent and/or vulnerable to share a piece of themselves. Normally, we are taught to tuck these pieces of us away in the closet. This doesn't mean to wear your heart on your sleeve. Quite the reverse. It is being able to discern when to disclose the right information to right person at the right time.

Whether we want to admit it or not, we will need ongoing help throughout this journey - and not just for homeschooling, but life in general. This reminds me of a mentoring program I had the privilege of being a part of called Titus 2. We were put into groups of three – one mentor, one mentee, and a prayer warrior. We scheduled times to meet and could decide between just chatting, doing a Bible study, devotional, or whatever. My first mentor and I decided to chat more than anything. And chatting was just what I needed at that time in my life. My second mentor and I decided to read through the book of John, and my goodness... that was exactly what I needed at *that* time in my life. The year and a half I spent part of this ministry taught me the importance of needing a support group. It showed me that I needed to be comfortable asking for help. And most of all, it showed me just how much this journey is **not** just about me.

When we humble ourselves, we never know who is watching, or who is listening (except our children). How other lives are touched is not up to us. All we can do is our best to always set good, godly examples for others to follow – especially our children. I wasn't going to talk much about the ripple effects of what asking for help can do because it's obvious that our children are watching our every move. They are listening to our every word spoken. To show our children that it is okay to ask for and receive help will only add to their character toolbelt.

How often do you find yourself saying, *"If I knew then what I know now."*? This is one of those topics I say that about quite a bit. I always express to my children that it is okay to ask for help. And even more so, it is even better when you accept the help. There are times when our son is headstrong and wants to do something without our help, only to end up coming to us and asking for it anyways. Instead of saying, *"I told you so!"* I use it as a future invitation to come and ask if he needs to, and without doubt or hesitation.

How much more do we need this in our adulthood? Ever so much! If we can just humble ourselves and say, *"You know what. I'm not sure where to start with homeschooling. Would you help point me in the right direction?"* Or, *"Hey, I'm struggling with choosing a curriculum. What are your thoughts about ---?"* It seems so simple to do, but you and I both know that's not always the case. In some instances, we would rather crash and burn than to ask for help. Let's stop that. Let's embrace the Titus 2 mentality and understand that we need support, and we need guidance. Not the comparing. Not the competition. Just togetherness.

Spiritual Tools

Whew, what a time we had today, beloved sister! I want us to promise each other that we will ask for help when needed. Will you promise that? We will both be better women because of it. As you read the next several pages, allow yourself to be receptive to what the Father wants to speak to you.

Be transformed by the renewing of your mind!

Limiting beliefs:

- I don't want to be a bother.
- I can do this by myself.
- I don't have a support circle/system.
- I'm hesitant on asking for help.
- I don't trust others.
- They probably can't help me anyways.

Affirmations:

- I will make it a point to develop a support circle/system.
- It is okay to ask for, and receive, help.
- I am showing my children a valuable characteristic.
- I will trust Yahweh to lead me to a good group of dependable friends/associates.
- I know others have been through what I am experiencing and can offer great advice.

Scripture for Meditation

Psalm 32:8 – "Let Me instruct you and teach you in the way you should go; let Me counsel, My eye be on you."

Psalm 34:5 – They looked to Him and were lightened, and their faces were not ashamed.

Psalm 121:1-2 – I life up my eyes to the hills; where does my help come from? My help comes from Yahweh, maker of the heavens and earth.

Provers 15:22 – Without counsel, plans go wrong, but by great counsellors they are established.

1 Thessalonians 5:11 – Therefore encourage one another, and build up one another, as indeed you do.

Let us pray,

Helpful Father. Thank You for Your Word. It reminds us that our help comes from You. It also encourages us to realize that we are also to help one another. We realize our lives are not simply for us to live for ourselves, or try to do by our self... but, it is to be lived in a way that impacts and helps others.

We pray that You would continue to send people in our lives who exhibit the Titus 2 mentality. Women that are strong in Your Word, and mighty in their actions in living for You. Give us the courage to reach out when we need to... to ask for help, and to receive the help that is provided for us.

We cannot and do not want to do this alone. May we continue to build one another up, encouraging each other wherever we may be in our unique journey's.

Cover my families with the wing of your protection. In the name of Yeshua our Messiah, amen.

Personal Reflections

✱ ✱ ✱ ✱ ✱ ✱

Staying true to your beliefs

In a world that is growing more and more secular with each passing day, it seems like compromise is knocking harder and harder at our front doors. *"Be okay with this,"* it says. *"Accept that,"* it demands. *"God would be okay if you did that,"* it whispers. Each time we give in and say, "Okay," it is another step closer to getting us further from staying true to our beliefs.

A growing trend I have seen in the homeschooling community is believers giving in to more secularism. Sometimes it's in the form of curriculum choice, while sometimes it's just flat out doing things they wouldn't normally do all in the name of blending or fitting in.

For our family, we have beliefs that cause us to stick out like a sore thumb. But instead of giving in, we stand firm. It doesn't mean that we are obnoxious about it, or make it a point to rub it in people's faces. No. We kindly turn down an engagement that may go against our beliefs, or choose not to do a certain curriculum because of the content it suggests teaching. It's that simple.

I've been homeschooling for 9 years and walking in Torah for 2 years. We continue to work with Christian curriculums and attend a Christian co-op. The beauty about homeschooling is that I modify every subject into what Torah says we should do. At co-op, we have shared the things we don't participate in and we are thankful that Abba has given us favor.
Yesenia E. - Algonquin, IL

I don't want this to be a chapter of telling you *what* you should believe in because we are all entitled to free will choice. I believe each person is held responsible for their own spiritual walk and must work out their own salvation. At the same time, it is my understanding that we can be stumbling blocks and hinder a person. But, surely that should never be our intention if we profess to believe in and follow the Most High.

Instead, what I want to do is encourage you to guard your beliefs. Guard the Word that you put into your mind and heart. Guard it enough to walk it out even when it seems tough. Even when the world around you says you that you are wrong, or that you can't believe that way. Stand firm. We are told over and over in Scripture to guard the Word of God, to be courageous, and to stand firm.

It should be no surprise that the world is getting worse as they days go by. According to Scripture, it is going to get even worse! I just didn't think it would get this bad so fast. But, there is no stopping it until the return of our King, our Messiah. In the meantime, we have instructions to endure. We have assignments to persevere. And we have tests to keep us on track. All of this is never just for us, but for those around us as well.

Speaking of which, it is so vital for our children to see us stand strong in what we believe. Not just talking about it, but living it. Doing this only adds to their character toolbelt (as I like to call it) which they will carry with them everywhere they go, and be a part of everything they do. We should not want to raise children who are master character-shifters (having the ability to easily conform to whatever is around them).

I've been there. Have you? I remember being a young child who was bullied and talked about because there were certain things I was not going to do. There was also a season as I began to get older where I would do what others did just to blend in. Perhaps it is a natural part of development; however, it doesn't have to be something that carries over into adulthood. Inevitably, that will carry over into our parenting, then into our children... who will then continue what was modeled for them.

Again, staying true to our beliefs isn't just about us, and it can extend far beyond our own families. People are watching, and people are waiting. They are watching and waiting for authenticity. That's one thing I pick up on more than anything about our Messiah. His authenticity. Of course, He is perfect. He did everything right. But what stands out to me more than anything is His authenticity in staying true to His beliefs and carrying out what the Father sent Him to do.

Sure, the story could have been different. He could have changed and aligned His life with what the Pharisees and Sadducees suggested that He should (or shouldn't) do. But He didn't. And He wasn't going to. What a huge lesson for us! We should choose to stand firm in times of being name-called, talked about, or even mistreated all while remaining authentic to what we believe. Never moved or shaken.

    My prayer is that we stay true to our beliefs for our children, and as examples to others who are watching and waiting. Because, my dear sweet sister... they are.

Spiritual Tools

Sister, I have a confession. I struggled with writing this chapter. I battled between keeping it, changing it, and taking it out completely. I wasn't sure how valid it would be. Then, I heard a still small voice tell me to leave it alone. I have faith that it spoke exactly how you needed to hear it. As you read the next several pages, I want you to remember the strength you have within you to stand firm in your beliefs.

Be transformed by the renewing of your mind!

Limiting beliefs:

- I don't want others to know I don't believe the same way.
- I don't want to draw attention because of my beliefs.
- It is hard to stand against the majority.
- I'm not sure what to say about my beliefs.
- It is easier to compromise.
- They will not accommodate to the way I believe.

Affirmations:

- I will not be ashamed of my beliefs.
- It is okay to stand strong in my beliefs.
- I am showing my children a valuable characteristic.
- I will trust Yahweh to protect me.
- I will not compromise my beliefs.

Scripture for Meditation

Deuteronomy 4:9 – "Only, guard yourself, and guard your life diligently, lest you forget the Words your eyes have seen, and lest they turn aside from your heart all the days of your life. And you shall make them known to your children and your grandchildren."

Romans 8:28 – And we know that all matters work together for good to those who love Elohim, to those who are called according to His purpose.

Romans 12:2 – And do not be conformed to this world, but be transformed by the renewing of your mind, so that you prove what is that good and well-pleasing and perfect desire of Elohim.

2 Corinthians 10:5 – Overthrowing reasonings and every high matter that exalts itself against the knowledge of Elohim, taking captive every thought to make it obedient to the Messiah.

Let us pray,

Unchanging Father. You are the same yesterday, today, and forever. Hallelujah! May that be an encouragement for us to never be moved and shaken from our beliefs… believing and living the Truth of Your everlasting Word.

We ask for strength in these times where compromise runs rapid. When our families are faced with the decision to compromise or accommodate, may we have the strength and courage to stand firm. Give us grace abundantly in those times, and mercy towards others.

May we never grow obnoxious or boastful in our beliefs, but never depreciate the confidence that comes with believing in the One True God.

Cover our families with the wing of your protection. In the name of Yeshua our Messiah, amen.

Personal Reflections

The sides.

Did you enjoy the meat portion? Normally, you may mix the meat and sides but for this meal, they needed to be separate. It's just *that* good! Now that we're ready to dive into our sides, let's switch gears. We talked about some deep stuff throughout the last few chapters, and now we are going to talk more about the surface of homeschooling. Time to grab the other fork and dig in.

* * * * * * *

There's a style for that

      Whether you realize it or not, every child has a learning style, and every teacher (that's you) has a teaching style. Homeschooling allows us the liberty to get it wrong, get it right, and switch it up anytime we need to. This freedom leads us to better understanding our child's unique learning style, and how to make learning (and teaching) more enjoyable.

      Here's another tidbit – you don't have to get it perfect. You don't have to get the curriculum perfect either. Truth be told, you don't have to choose just one at all. Styles, curricula, and supplements simply exist to make teaching and learning a bit easier (okay, maybe a lot easier). I know of several moms, including myself, who pull a little from this, and a little from that. There are others who have found their rainbow curriculum in form of the already put together boxes. And for them, it works from beginning to end.

When it comes to these features, there are many to choose from. However, let's break down the varying learning styles first. Often, we are not aware of our children's learning style, and this can be what stands in the way of having a totally successful homeschool journey. You may also be shocked to realize that you may have a combination of learning styles too. Below is a quick overview:

Style	Characteristics/Preferences
Aural	Enjoys working to sound and music
Logical	Drawn to logic and reasoning systems
Physical	Using body, hands, and sense of touch
Social	Learns best in group settings
Solitary	Likes working alone and the use of self-study
Verbal	Enjoys words, both in speech and writing
Visual	Drawn to pictures, images, and special understanding

Ever wonder why your child likes to listen to music while completing book work, and jumps for excitement upon hearing the words *"co-op?"* Perhaps it is because he/she is an aural-social learner. Hopefully this chart will help you better understand your child's learning style.

Learning about the various styles of learning was one of my favorite subjects in college. Once I began working in the classroom setting, I could really begin to understand and see them in action. What was difficult, though, was learning how to accommodate the varying learning style of so many children grouped together in one class. Insert the sigh of relief of not having to homeschool 20+ children (unless you have a ginormous family).

On the upside, understanding how your child learns will only increase your ability to teach them in a way that works for them. Sometimes, the downside is having multiple children, with multiple learning styles, stretched across different ages and grades. Don't get nervous though... we will talk about this more in the next chapter.

Now that we have broken down the learning styles, let's look at how these styles fit within methods used by many homeschoolers. I've included another chart to summarize them:

Method	Summary
Charlotte Mason	Learning through play, creating, and involvement in real-life situations.
Classical Conversations	Combines at-home learning with weekly classroom experiences taught by tutor-trained parents.
Montessori	Emphasizes error-less learning. Children learn at own pace. Discourages TV and computers.
Multiple Intelligences	Adapts scheduling and materials to bring out and work with child's natural strengths.
Relaxed/Eclectic	A little of this and that. Formal mornings, relaxed afternoons with specific times.
School-at-Home	Most expensive with the highest burnout rate. Usually involves boxed curricula, set schedules, strict routines.
Unschooling	Natural, interest-led, and child-led learning. Embraces freedom.
Waldorf	Focuses on educating the whole child: mind, body, and spirit. Doesn't use standard textbooks.

Looking at the chart, you may find a variety of methods that work for you. A few homeschooling moms I have talked to use Classical Conversations and the Montessori method. *Most* moms I've talked to about methods have admitted to using a variety of the ones listed above… usually a mix of relaxed and unschooling, with a touch of school-at-home if they purchase a boxed curriculum.

A newer homeschooling mom may dabble with just one method at a time. The seasoned mom may purposefully implement more than one to accommodate varying learning styles. Keep in mind that you should choose whatever works for you whether it has a jazzy name or not.

Most people call me a Classical Unschooler.
Melinda G. - Philadelphia, PA

Our family uses a mix of Waldorf with our own twist and relaxed/eclectic simply because I have yet to purchase an actual boxed curriculum. We don't have a concrete daily schedule that we abide by. And, I use a lot of free printables with hand-me-down textbooks. Speaking of not having a strict daily schedule, I'll go into more detail about scheduling and planning in another chapter.

Nevertheless, understanding styles and methods come in handy especially when your choice for homeschooling involves some sort of exceptionality (ADD/ADHD, dyslexia, cognitive regression, etc.). In the most recent days, public and private schools have moved toward less accommodation to students with any kind of exception while still trying to practice classroom inclusion. This has been proven to not be so feasible for most students, and it leaves parents frustrated with narrowed options.

My child was diagnosed with ADHD. The teachers kept pushing for medication instead of finding alternate ways to keep her attention during class.
Shateeka O. – Hopkinsville, KY

Regardless of the reasons behind *why* we choose to homeschool, it is comforting to know that there are labeled styles and methods that can guide us in helping our children learn by ways that best suite them. If you already know and implement styles and methods, great! If you are new and have no clue what to do, I recommend researching the styles and methods mentioned in more depth.

There are free online tests (one mentioned in the homeschool toolbox at the end of the book) to check learning styles, and tons of other reliable online resources. Most of the methods have websites that will send more information in the form of pamphlets or packets. Not to mention, there are numerous support groups in the form of blogs, forums, and Facebook groups.

Be sure to give yourself, and your child, time as you figure out what works best for you both. It may take a year of curriculum mess-ups before finding one that works for you. It may take months of teaching style switch-ups before understanding what makes the right connection. Homeschooling offers us the freedom and ability for this so take advantage of it!

Don't get discouraged. Stay confident in knowing this is all part of the process. Keep in mind that you are making the best decisions possible for your children. Don't hesitate to utilize that support circle we talked about a couple chapters ago too. It is stress relieving knowing that you can reach out to other moms who have tried a variety of styles, methods, curriculum, and supplements.

My local homeschool group is amazing at tossing ideas around. We freely ask what has worked, and what hasn't. This group has also gone as far as to establish support meetings for moms with exceptional children. It is this kind of support that helps smooth out the bumps that come along with homeschooling.

Yes, there is a lot of information out there, but don't allow yourself to get overwhelmed. Research a little here, and try a little there. Never be afraid of change. Just keep putting one foot in front of the other, always moving forward.

Never underestimate the curiosity and creativity in children.
Angela H. - Cincinnati, OH

Spiritual Tools

Isn't it comforting to know that we all have our own style? There may be labels coined on the varying forms that are out there, but how encouraging is it to know they all came from our Heavenly Father? As you read over the next several pages, may you be reassured in knowing that you and your family's originality is no surprise to Yahweh. He blessed you with the varying abilities that make up your family, and they are especially for y'all!

Be transformed by the renewing of your mind!

Limiting beliefs:

- I don't understand my children.
- I can't reach my child.
- My teaching style is not working.
- My child shuts down when learning something new.
- I don't know how to accommodate my child's way of learning.

Affirmations:

- I will take time to understand my children.
- I will find unique ways to reach my unique children.
- My children are special and deserve the best education I can provide.
- I will take time to try different teaching styles.
- I will learn the best method(s) for teaching my children.

Scripture for Meditation

Psalm 28:7 – Yahweh is my strength, and my shield; my heart has trusted in Him, and I have been helped; therefore my heart exults, and with my song I thank Him.

Psalm 139:14-15 – I give thanks to You, for I am awesomely and wondrously made! Wondrous are Your works, and my being knows it well. My bones were not concealed from You, when I was shaped in a hidden place, knit together in the depths of the earth.

Ephesians 2:10 – For we are His workmanship, created in Messiah Yeshua unto good works, which Elohim prepared beforehand that we should walk in them.

Let us pray,

Incredible Father. We are forever thankful for Your wondrous works. Thank You for making each of our children unique and awesome in their own ways. Give us the wisdom to embrace how they were created.

We ask for grace as we lead, guide, and direct them according to Your Word, and the path you have set before them. Help us to understand each of our children in their own gifting's and abilities, always seeking to uplift and encourage them.

You are the Master Creator, so it is You from whom we draw our strength, courage, and patience. We welcome this journey of learning about our children with an open heart, open eyes, and open arms.

Cover our families with the wing of your protection. In the name of Yeshua our Messiah, amen.

Personal Reflections

✱ ✱ ✱ ✱ ✱ ✱ ✱ ✱ ✱

The multiple struggle

Homeschooling multiple children who are different ages, in different grades, and with varying learning style, needs, and abilities is truly a gift – not a burden. The looks and comments glared your way when you tell people that you homeschool while looking at your tribe of children would suggest otherwise. But, we know it is totally a blessing. I used to think people were crazy to have large families, but as I've begun to acquire a herd of my own, I genuinely see the blessing.

Before we get into the meat and potatoes of the multiple struggle, we must deal with the heart strings first. There are dynamics to consider, and when taken into consideration, they can be used as fuel. Families with multiple children will experience the need to meet more individual needs, emotional needs, learning needs, and educational needs multiplied by how ever many members there are in the family. This isn't something to be feared! Instead of allowing it to seem like a tornado, let's focus on building a structure to withstand the storms. Because let's face it, the waves will come.

    Although it is easier said than done, being patient, flexible, and having expectations will help build a sturdy foundation. Add a dose of discipline, and you will be well-equipped for an environment that may tend to get a little hectic at times. It is to be expected; however, it does not have to burn all your energy and end in more days wasted than saved.

    After tying heart strings, it is important to forget the status quo. Forget what people are saying, and ignore unreliable suggestions about how you should be teaching *your* children. Instead, focus on teaching your children where they are. Take time to do a mental rundown of how your children learn best, and your preferred teaching style. If you are like me, this is something I would have to write down. If you do choose to write it down, consider adding it to your homeschool planning binder, if you use one, and update as necessary.

We talked about styles in more detail in the last chapter, and as we discovered, there are many learning styles and methods. Find what works for you, your children, and everyone collectively. It can be a lot easier if you have an idea about your teaching style and ways your children learn best before diving into much else. I came across an amazing learning style quiz that is noted in the resources section at the end of the book. Take that quiz for each of your children to help get an idea of their learning style, and go from there. Knowing this can help you plan and prepare to teach multiple children with less stress.

You know how the saying goes – *If you fail to plan, you plan to fail.* This doesn't mean you need to plan a homeschool boot camp, but it does mean having some sort of structure. I recommend starting by making a generic schedule. If the word schedule scares you, make a chart. Keep in mind that this is not the detailed minute by minute for the next four weeks kind of schedule (or chart). We will get into that in the next chapter. For now, just know that having a basic schedule, or chart, is a great start.

Another misconception is when you are teaching multiple children, you must be all over the place, all the time. This does not have to be the case, and you don't have to do more work than you need to. If you haven't done the research already, you may be shocked at just how many ideas there are about ways to homeschool multiple kiddos. Too many to name, but we are going to talk about a few that hold top spots on the overall list.

Integrated learning is one of the most common ways moms homeschool multiple children. This also takes the name of group learning, group time, family learning, and/or circle time. Basically, all the children are learning and participating together. This is a perfect way to do collective praying, Bible reading, concept and lesson introduction, and whatever else you want to do. I personally like this way because I can maintain what would normally turn into a hectic situation while still focusing on individual children when needed.

Group learning also makes for a smooth transition into independent learning, if you have children able to do that. Independent learning doesn't necessarily start at a certain age or grade. It is more dependent on the level of maturity. As a mile marker, it can start once a child is able to read and comprehend directions. Now, it doesn't mean responsibility with no deadlines or supervision... even as an adult, I still need deadlines and some supervision, don't you?

Some parents find that independent learning is made easier with Sue Patrick's workbox system. This particular system has various advantages beyond increasing a child's self-control, independence, and learning, which we will discuss in a later chapter. The main goals of the workbox system are: to create ways to present curriculum to our children in ways that are inviting and make sense to them; enhance teaching angles that offer more effective teaching; and, help the child be more focused while completing work successfully and independently. Again, we will look at the detail of this in a later chapter.

When independent work isn't the best option, consider what I call the double-up method. This means teaching the same subject, at the same time, to all children. The only difference is the level of work and understanding will vary. This is like circle time, or group learning but is more subject focused versus "start of the day activities" focused. I normally use this method with unit studies because I can read something, then follow up with worksheets, activities, or videos that are tailored to each of my children's age and grade.

With today's technology, using online curriculum is another way to manage multiple ages. This will also take a little bit of independent learning, but can be an amazing tool. We have found several online programs that allow our son to work at his individual level, and the pace is customized to his needs. The best part is they are **free**, and in the homeschool toolbox resource section at the end of the book.

    Having an environment conducive to homeschooling multiple grades is a plus as well. When there are different ages and grades represented, it can help create a sense of togetherness and collective learning. As my children get older, posters change, color schemes change, even the way I position things around the room(s) change. As of writing this book, we live in a small two-bedroom duplex, so our homeschool environment is spread between the living room, kitchen, and our oldest son's room. You may have one school room, or school all over the place too, but we can still provide a setup that compliments schooling multiple children no matter the space or place.

    Along with choosing what works for you, remember to map out your children's progress often. You may have an instance where two children are ready to learn the same concept. For example, my one one-year-old and two-year-old have been, and will most likely continue, learning together until they show otherwise. You may have a second and third grader who are learning times tables together. Take advantage of that! There may also be times where your older children can help with the younger ones, which will only reiterate concepts they have previously learned.

While talking about these teaching multiple children ideas, remember to be open for change. You may find that a piece of this method works combined with another piece from another method. Perhaps it only works for one semester. Don't hesitate to switch things up, and continue accommodating as you see fit.

If something is not working for you child, you have the power to make adjustments at any time.
Angela H. – Cincinnati, OH

Finding a system that works is certainly a process. It is easy to get lost in piecing this together, and breaking that apart, but let us not forget to take care of ourselves. Our "me-time" gets stretched enough between having multiple kids, caring for them, taking care of the home, cooking, cleaning, etc. Let us also plan for a moment to ourselves, whether it be early morning quiet time with the Father, or a relaxing bath before bedtime. Just make sure it's really late so the kids don't wake up. You are supermom, indeed; but even a superhero needs downtime. So, don't feel guilty about planning that for yourself!

Spiritual Tools

Sweet sister, we sure are blessed. Aren't we? Whether we have just one child or several, it is an amazing calling. I hope you are inspired with a new way of seeing homeschooling multiple children. Indeed, it can be a struggle, but there isn't a struggle too big that our Creator King can't help us with. As you read over the next several pages, keep that mind.

Be transformed by the renewing of your mind!

Limiting beliefs:

- I don't know how I am going to do this.
- I can't figure out how to do this.
- My children are not working well together (or separate).
- I'm at my wits end.
- I don't know how to accommodate my children's varying needs.

Affirmations:

- I will take time to understand my children.
- I will find unique ways to teach my unique children.
- My children are learning how to work well together.
- I will take time to learn about different ways to homeschool multiple children.
- My children are blessed to have one another.

Scripture for Meditation

Deuteronomy 6:6-8 – "And these Words which I am commanding you today shall be in your heart, and you shall impress them upon your children, and shall speak of them when you sit in your house, and when you walk by the way, and when you lie down, and you rise up, and shall bind them as a sign on your hand, and they shall be as frontlets between your eyes."

Isaiah 41:13 – "For I, Yahweh your Elohim, am strengthening your right hand, saying to you, 'Do not fear, I shall help you.'"

Ecclesiastes 3:1 – For every matter there is an appointed time, even a time for every pursuit under the heavens.

Let us pray,

Loving Father. Your ways are above our ways, and Your thoughts are above our thoughts; therefore, we will seek You in our times of need. You have blessed us with one of life's most precious gifts – a piece of Your heritage… our children.

It is our heart's desire to raise our children in a way that glorifies and honors You, while blessing them. We will teach them Your Word, how to meditate on it, and most important, how to walk it out.

We understand the season we are in… one of raising several children at the same time, and oh what a blessing. Thank you for allowing us to be a vessel and a tool to raise children for Your Kingdom.

Cover our families with the wing of your protection. In the name of Yeshua our Messiah, amen.

Personal Reflections

✸ ✸ ✸ ✸ ✸ ✸ ✸ ✸ ✸

Paging Mrs. Secretary

I could sum this chapter up in one word: Pinterest. However, beyond the thousands of pins related to homeschool planning and organizing, we still need to find a system that works for us and put it into practice. Sounds simple, doesn't it? For some, maybe. For others, not so much. Planning and organizing your homeschool is probably top on the stress list, if not number one. Then again, it doesn't have to be that way. Embrace the process and take it one step at a time.

It is a given that without planning and organization we will be running a circus act and selling tickets to the next show. As mentioned in the last chapter, if we fail to plan, we are basically planning to fail. Now, if you haven't caught the underlying thread of this entire book, I'll repeat it again:

Find (and do) what works best for you and your family, changing however much you need to!

There is no secret formula, no extended equation to figure out, and no one set way. This is about finding your sweet spot and running with it. Homeschooling runs so much smoother for me when the planning and organizing is working. It gives me a sort of energy boost, and always helps me start the year with great confidence. Of course, there have been times where my plan of actions, and even the way I organized, crash within the first couple of months. But that's the joy of being able to switch it up.

It is also a blessing that we have hundreds and thousands of ideas at our fingertips (thank you, Google). The fact that others want to share what has worked for them, and make it readily available for others to use, validates that we are all in this together. We are all aboard the same train, even if we are in different cars.

In this chapter, we will dive deep into the planning and organizing aspects of homeschooling. I'd like to start by sharing the steps I took from the beginning; then, I'll ask some questions for you to answer. We will then take those questions and plug in some methods that may be a good fit for planning and organizing your homeschool year (and years to come).

My 7-step method for starting homeschooling:

1. **Make the choice to do it.** This isn't always easy. It can be a back-and-forth thing. Maybe because you want to homeschool, but the husband isn't so sure. Or, perhaps the lack of resources keeps you hesitant on making the leap. Whatever the case, the first step is to decide you want to do it.
2. **Look up state laws.** Each state is different; therefore, it is wise to know early on what your state requires of you and for you to homeschool. I live in Kentucky, so it is relatively easy to homeschool here. No annual testing, no pop-up visits, no presenting before a board, and so on. Find out what your state requires and don't let it stop you from homeschooling.
3. **Make necessary contacts to unenroll children from public/private schools/institutions.** This is a very important step to do early on. In most cases, a call to the local board of education can lead you in the right direction. Give yourself plenty of time to do what is required for this step. Be sure to ask if it is something that you are required to do yearly.

4. **Establish a schedule/routine.** This involves whipping out the calendar and deciding: when do you want to start? When do you want to end? What days do you want to take off in between for holidays, vacations, breaks, etc.? Do you want to teach certain subjects on certain days? Do you want to school four days a week? Half days? School all year (on eight weeks, off two weeks, for example)? This is totally up to your discretion. Just be sure it coincides with your state's laws about how many days per year (or hours) a child is to be "schooled."
5. **Research curriculum and resources.** Each year, I really enjoy doing this step because there is so much that exists for the homeschooling community. From Google to Pinterest, you will quickly find any and everything you could possibly think of (or not) to use as part of your homeschooling. I also take this time to establish a budget, and decide if we were going to purchase curriculum, use free curriculum, or a combination of that and creating my own. Four years of homeschooling so far and I have yet to purchase an actual curriculum. Most of my purchases go to supplements to complement what curriculum I have come up with.

6. **Search for local support.** This is huge. I was shocked (again) to find that our little ol' hometown had a thriving homeschool group, faith-based at that, which is a plus for us. I would not have found this group had I stayed in my little box thinking that homeschooling was still old-school and nobody really does it. Since I started with that group, it has double in size! And that's not all. If you type in the word "homeschool" in the Facebook search bar, you will get a homeschool group for **everything** you could think of. The support is out there. Homeschooling is not a secret society that people are scared to talk about.

7. **Pray, and get started.** It would be horrible to do all the planning, all the scheduling, all the preparation, only to never get started. If you've made it to this step, there is nothing left for you to do but pray and leap. Whatever day you established as your first day of school, stick with it. Anticipate the day. Make a fun countdown, especially if it's your first year. Have a not-back-to-school party, homeschool style. Our homeschool group does this and it is always a blast. There are tons of ways to make it fun!

Now that I've shared my seven-step method with you, I'd like for you to answer some questions to get your planning and organizing gears going. Then, we will follow up with some methods to try (if you haven't tried them already).

7 Questions to get Your Gears Going

These are questioned pulled from my seven-step method but put in a way for your personal reflection:

1. Have you made the choice to homeschool?
2. Are you familiar with your state's laws? Have you printed them out and filed them with other important homeschool information?
3. Do you have a plan in place to unenroll you children from public/private school? Do you have to do it yearly?
4. Have you started researching curriculum and resources? What are your favorites?
5. Have you established a schedule/routine?
6. Do you have local support?
7. Are you doing anything special to celebrate getting started?

While this certainly is not an exhausted list of questions you could ask yourself, it is a great place to start. It will get you thinking about your planning preferences, and lead to more questions, such as:

- Do you like simple, summarized, or detailed planning?
- Do you like having your plans kept in folders, binders, hung on the wall for all to see, etc.?
- How will you schedule your days?
- Are you participating in extra-curricular activities, co-op groups, library programs, etc.?
- Will you use a system to help plan your individual homeschool days?
- How/Where will you store homeschool supplies, materials, supplements, etc.
- Will there be a set work space, homeschooling room, or area(s) that you primarily school in?

See how the hamster wheel starts to spin? One question can surely spark another, and no question that comes to mind should be dismissed. Everything you could think to ask most likely means it will be important to your homeschooling journey. So, ask and find an answer for it.

Let's discuss a couple of approaches to planning and organizing:

The simple approach

If you prefer a simple approach to planning, you may like the flow chart system. A flow chart is a guide of what to do next, without the restrictions of having to note exactly when something will be done. A flow chart can be a peacekeeper in the home of schooling multiple children. Why? Because you can make a simple list that also takes into consideration each person in the home. I use a flow chart to pre-plan:

Huddleston Academy Flow Chart

Wake up/Breakfast/Clean
Family Group Learning
Spelling/Grammar
Reading & Comprehension
Math
Lunch/Cleanup/Rest
Social Studies/Geography
Science/History
Specials
Free time

The simple approach to organizing looks a lot like file folders, accordion folders (the one with multiple pockets), filing cabinets, and boxes. Again, there is no wrong way to organize. Some moms struggle with organization because they feel like it must be some perfect process... one that we know doesn't exist. What makes it "perfect" is the fact that you have found something that works for you.

The summary approach

For the moms who like to summarize her planning and scheduling, the flow chart can be built upon, or skipped altogether. A summary usually consists of a little detail that may include concepts you want to teach, times of the day you want to school, notes of curriculum you may want to use, and so on. There is no right or wrong way to summarize planning and organizing for your homeschool. Here's an example of how I build on my flow chart:

Huddleston Academy
Flow Chart w/ Summary Example

Family Group Learning
- Bible/Hebrew
    o Memory verse (1 per week)
    o Hebrew alphabet
    o Hebrew numbers
    o Hebrew colors
    o Beginner Hebrew words
    o Use Pre-K/4th gd. Workbooks
- Calendar/Weather
    o Calendar chart
    o Look outside daily
    o Weather chart
    o Use/read thermometer
    o Group seasonal activities

The detailed approach

A detailed layout is what I end up with by the time I have finished charting and summarizing. I like having details of what I want the children to do daily, but I don't go as far as to slap times on it. This is something I tried in the beginning and could not get to work for anything. Funny thing though, I still have a "time schedule" in my homeschool planning binder. I should probably take that out now. In the meantime, here is a sample picture of my weekly lesson plan chart. This can be found on my blog which is notated in the homeschool toolbox:

Weekly Lesson Plan
Week Of: August 14 - 18

Subject	Monday	Tuesday	Wednesday	Thursday	Friday
Bible Hebrew	Torah Portion Psalm 119	--------> -------->			Test & Review
Spelling English	Week 1 words Parts of Sent.	Synonyms Parts of Sent.	Definitions	Rainbow	
Math	Times tables	-------->			
Science Social Studies	Creation Community	--------> -------->			

©Michelle Huddleston

Some moms do detail planning for weeks, months, a semester, or even a year in advance. This may be easier to do if you are using a boxed curriculum that comes with everything already mapped out for you. Even then, there is still some overview planning to factor in just in case you need to switch things up, replace, or re-pace. I set a goal to plan at least two weeks to a month ahead of time. In my opinion, planning for unit studies or repetitive concept teaching makes planning more relaxing.

There is a system I brought up in the last chapter that I'd like to highlight, especially if you are homeschooling multiple children. Sue Patrick's workbox system. The idea behind this system is mainly to aid in creating independent children with self-control. This is accomplished because children know what is expected of them each day. At any time, they can see how much work is left to be completed, and they do not have to guess when the school day is over.

This system is accomplished by using ten to twelve section storage carts to separate each subject's work that is to be completed for the day. Included in each section are all the materials needed to complete the lesson. If you are short on space, try using something as basic as a hanging space organizer.

Sue also uses a strategic way of having children keep up with the work they have complete. One mom mentioned that she changed this process for her homeschool and her children do much better with what she swapped in its place. That is what stands out most about her system. The fact that it can be tweaked to accommodate your unique homeschooling needs makes it a very reliable resource.

A system like Susan's does require some form of detailed organization. When it comes to this type of organization, it may look like book shelves, storage bins, lots of cart-drawer bins, binders, and spiral bounds. The detailed organizer likes everything to have a place, usually labeled, and used for specific purposes. Living in a two-bedroom duplex, I am *very* detailed when it comes to organization. Thankfully, there are hundreds of pins on Pinterest that give amazing ideas for those schooling in the smallest of spaces to the largest of spaces.

I don't want to exhaust you on the numerous ways to plan and organize; but, hopefully you have a starting point. Most importantly, I want you to have a boost in confidence to find your planning and organizing niche! Be secure in what you choose! You got this mom!

Spiritual Tools

We talked about quite a bit today, didn't we? As you read over the next several pages, I want you to keep in mind that there is no right or wrong way to plan and organize your homeschool. Walk in the confidence of the choices you make.

Be transformed by the renewing of your mind!

Limiting beliefs:

- I don't know where to begin planning and organizing.
- It overwhelms me to think about planning.
- I am not good at keeping anything organized.
- I don't know where to start.
- My days are hectic and chaotic.
- I am afraid to change or try anything new.

Affirmations:

- There are resources available to help me.
- I will be confident in how I plan and organize my homeschool.
- My homeschool will function with grace and ease.
- I am not afraid of change.
- What I choose to do is in my family's best interests.

Scripture for Meditation

Psalm 20:4 - He does give you according to your heart, and fills all your plans.

Psalm 143:8 - Let me hear Your loving-commitment in the morning, for in You I have put my trust; let me know the way in which I should walk, for I have lifted up my being to You.

Proverbs 16:3 - Commit your works to Yahweh, and your plans shall be established.

Proverbs 16:9 - A man's heart plans his way, but Yahweh establishes his steps.

Let us pray,

Unchanging Father. We commit all our plans to You. We cannot do anything without You, and we wouldn't want it any other way. Your Word says you establish our steps, and our plans. For that, we are thankful.

Give us the knowledge and wisdom to plan and organize in a way that is glorifying to You, and a blessing to my family. Show us areas that we need improvement in, giving us grace to accept when changes need to be made.

Thank You for giving us the desires of our hearts to homeschool our children.

Cover our families with the wing of your protection. In the name of Yeshua our Messiah, amen.

Personal Reflections

✳ ✳ ✳ ✳ ✳ ✳ ✳ ✳ ✳ ✳

Forget the first day

If you have made it this far, whoo-hoo! Now I want to share some advice you may have never heard before...

FORGET THE FIRST DAY!

At this point, you have done all the planning and organizing your mind and hands can suffice. The curriculum is set. You've brainstormed and mapped out your year. The pencils are sharpened, and the supplies area is stocked. You are ready.

The first day comes and the kids don't want to get out of bed. You're not so sure about kicking the day off like you originally planned, and it ends up taking two hours to get started. One child asks a million questions, while the other pouts about school starting so soon, and you're chasing a toddler who woke up and decided she didn't like coloring anymore. You manage to get the kids in order while sipping on a cup of coffee that is now ice cold. At the end of the school day you managed to get the little one to color, half of the million questions answered, and the other says it wasn't so bad after all. Congratulations, mom! You have just successfully completed your first day of homeschool.

Now pat yourself on the back and do a little jive! Then, forget about it. Why do I say forget the first day? Because first days are not the real indicators of how the rest of your homeschool year will go. If we allow it to do that, we can end up with a defeated mindset as soon as something goes wrong. A defeated mindset will resist change, neglect to see things differently, and end up burnt out before ever seeing the real blessings of homeschooling.

The most seasoned homeschool mom will admit that all first days are different. Just like every pregnancy is different, so is each homeschool year. That's why I have repeatedly said to not only do what works for you and your family, but also embrace change. As our children grow, they change. The more experiences we have adults, we change. The same principle can be applied to each individually unique homeschool. The longer you homeschool, the more you understand the concept of individuality and transformation.

Each year, the doubts will arise. Questions will flood your thoughts. And the process of rebooting will start all over again. Then again, that's where we remember that we are 98% mom and 2% teacher. We take care of our children's heart strings before anything else; and, we let our natural abilities to love and nurture ring out.

When our worst enemy tries to whisper lies to set up doubt and fear, we remind her that we are trusting in Yahweh with all our heart, leaning not on our own understanding. The no soliciting sign comes out, and the rent is cancelled on the space she wants to rent in our heads. Our worst enemy will not get the final say in our journey.

When the hard days come, and they will, we face them head on with anticipation to learn something new. The hard days, and all that is wrapped in them, will be cast on Yahweh because we know He will sustain us. These days do not get the final say either. Hard days teach us how to keep pushing, and to keep putting one foot in front of the other.

When the fix-all mentality comes with all its glitz and glamour, it gets the boot too. Remember that nine times out of ten, we don't know what's really going on behind that Facebook post, Pinterest pin, or latest new blog post. What we see is the finished product, the latest free printable to try, and the newest activity to incorporate. Homeschool moms everywhere go through the same struggles. So, don't get caught up in the "if I do it like that it'll fix it all" mentality. Remember to **trust**. Trust Yahweh and trust yourself in this process.

    When you need help, don't hesitate to ask. Helping one another is so important on this journey, and it very well could save a mom from making an irrational decision based off emotions instead of reality. Emotions are very real, don't get me wrong. But you know like I know, emotions can play tricks on us, especially if we don't have control over them. Help is there. Just ask. Receive. And do.

    When you are faced with opposition, never compromise your beliefs. Stay true to them, never wavering. Remember to guard yourself and guard your life diligently. Don't forget the Word your eyes have seen, and make them known to your children and grandchildren. Standing firm in your beliefs has such a great impact, primarily on your children, but also to others as well. You never know who is watching and waiting for someone just like you.

    Never forget there's a style for that. Whether "that" is a child who easily gets distracted, or thrives when music is played, there are learning and teaching styles that can help you throughout your homeschooling journey. Remember the change that will take place over the years too. It is normal and totally okay! Accommodation will be your new best friend. Trust me.

If you have the blessed struggle of homeschooling multiple children, whatever you do, don't give up. Yahweh your Elohim promises to strengthen you and says to not fear because He will help you. Find a few Scriptures that are your go-to in the time of anxiousness. Consider using the tried and true methods of other homeschooling moms until you find your sweet spot. Then, run with it!

When it's time to summon Mrs. Secretary, wear that hat with confidence. You know there is much planning and organizing ahead, but you can do it. You can do all things through Yeshua Messiah who gives you strength. You've already chosen to delight yourself in Yahweh, therefore let Him give you the desires of your heart. All homeschool moms desire to homeschool or we wouldn't be doing it. Wrapped in that too is the desire to be the best mother and teacher we can be. Let Yahweh bless you in that.

Finally, when the first day comes, whether it went as planned or totally flopped, forget about it. Keep pushing, and keep moving forward. Stay focused on your calling as a wife, mother, and homeschooler.

Savor the season you are in and embrace its goodness. I genuinely hope this book has blessed your socks off, and that you'll revisit it time and time again. I'm here for you, praying with you, and homeschooling along with you. We are in this together sister, and it is my heart's desire to see us all glorify the Father and reap the blessings from the seeds we've sown along the way.

Until next time, be blessed my dear sweet sister…

Spiritual Tools

I have thoroughly enjoyed our time together, sweet sister. As you read over the next several pages, I encourage you to really press into understanding that you were called to do this. You were called to be a Proverbs 31 woman, wife, and mother. All that is included with this role is meant to equip you to live victoriously and confidently.

Be transformed by the renewing of your mind!

Limiting beliefs:

- My first day was horrible, hopefully this isn't a sign of how the rest of the year will go.
- The first day was so overwhelming.
- I was not prepared.
- I don't know what I'm doing, and my first day proved that.
- I don't know where I went wrong.
- This isn't going to work.

Affirmations:

- Every first day is different and unique.
- I will not let the first day be an indicator of how the rest of the year will go.
- First days are needed to get started.
- I am doing what is best for my family.
- We are blessed to be able to homeschool.

Scripture for Meditation

Psalm 37:4 – And delight yourself in Yahweh, and let Him give you the desires of your heart.

Colossians 3:15 – And let the peace of Elohim rule in your hearts, to which indeed you were called in one Body, and be filled with thanks.

Hebrews 11:1 – And belief is the substance of what is expected, the proof what is not seen.

1 Peter 5:7 – Cast all your worry upon Him, for he is concerned about you.

Let us pray,

Abba Father. You have been so good to us. We cannot begin to count the number of blessings. May we never forget throughout this homeschooling journey that it is a blessing within itself. We know you will continue to sustain us and our families because You care for us.

You have not and will not lead us astray. We put our trust in You completely. You are our Rock, our Redeemer, our Restorer, and our Comforter.

Help us stay encouraged throughout this journey, never forgetting the bigger picture. We know it's not about us, but also about our children, our family, and others who will be impacted by the lives we live. Thank You for all you do Abba.

Cover our families with the wing of your protection. In the name of Yeshua our Messiah, amen.

Personal Reflections

The dessert.

I hope you have enjoyed your meal thus far. Do you still have room for dessert? I hope so, because your meal is not quite over yet. Now is the time to enjoy the final treat. This section is packed with reliable references, a homeschool toolbox that has lots of valuable information and resources, and information to get connected with me. There is also space for you to notate any resources you find too. Enjoy!

Homeschool toolbox (Resources)

Throughout the book, I made several references to which you will find detailed information about in this section. I have also noted some amazing blogs that offer resourceful information that will surely compliment your homeschooling journey. You will also find useful information about homeschooling laws and other valuable information.

Each state has different laws and requirements about homeschooling. Below, you will find websites that offer up-to-date information and legal resources:

Home School Legal Defense Association
www.hslda.org

Coalition for Responsible Home Education
www.responsiblehomeschooling.org

The following blogs and websites have great resources for homeschooling:

My personal blog, With the Huddleston's, offers a wealth of homeschooling information from how to get started to free curriculum and printables.
www.withthehuddlestons.com
www.facebook.com/withthehuddlestons

Heidi Cooper is the face and voice behind Torah Family Living – a website dedicated to helping families make Torah the heart of their home. She offers Torah portion ideas and resources, as well as free printables and curriculum supplements for purchase.
www.torahfamilyliving.com
www.facebook.com/torahfamilyliving

Lynn Hegedus is the creator of LH Education and specializes in several educational services, materials shipped straight to your door, as well as coaching and consulting services.
www.lheducation.org
www.facebook.com/LHEdu4U

The Learning Style Quiz I mentioned came from this amazing blog:
www.hiphomeschoolingblog.com/the-learning-style-quiz/

More information about Sue Patrick's workbox system can be found here:
www.workboxsystem.com

If you are looking for inexpensive, discounted, and free homeschool curriculum, supplements, resources, and supplies - check these websites:

Amazon
www.amazon.com

Christian Book
www.christianbook.com

Discount School Supply
www.discountschoolsupply.com

Easy Peasy All-in-One Homeschool
allinonehomeschool.com

Exodus Books
www.exodusbooks.com

Homeschooling Torah
http://tinyurl.com/htwithus

Rainbow Resource Center
www.rainbowresource.com

Ideas for homeschool planning an organizing can be found on these websites:

Pinterest
www.pinterest.com

Homeschool Ideas
www.homeschooling-ideas.com

A Peak Inside my Homeschool Planning Binder
https://youtu.be/OqJafODxcWg
*I mention several blogs that I pulled free printables from to make by planning binder for 2017-2018:
- The Relaxed Homeschool
- Blessed Learners
- New Beginnings
- Simply Preschool
- The Frugal Homeschool Mom

Early in the book I mentioned a life and business strategist. There are also homeschool coaches available to help throughout your journey.

Gary Coxe, Life & Business Strategist
garycoxe.com

7 Sisters Homeschool Coaching
7sistershomeschool.com/coaching/

The Homeschool Alliance, Coaching with Julie Bogart
coachjuliebogart.com

References

Special thanks to the following homeschooling moms for providing their words of encouragement and inspiration:

Melinda G.
Gina G.
Angela H.
Shateeka O.
Faith S.
Yesenia E.

Coxe, Gary. (2006). Don't Let Others Rent Space in Your Head. Hoboken, New Jersey: John Wiley & Sons, Inc.

Patrick, Sue. (2008). Sue Patrick's Workbox System: A User's Guide. Wake Forest, North Carolina: Wend Publishing, LLC.

As you come across resources, notate to them below:

Resource	Purpose	Website

Resource	Purpose	Website

Contact the author

Michelle desires to inspire and empower women to walk confidently in their calling. Her life experiences, both good and bad, have led her into a deeper relationship with Yeshua Messiah and Yahweh our Elohim. She loves spreading the love of Yahweh with all she encounters.

Are you interested in having Michelle speak at your event? Michelle is available to speak at congregations, MOPs groups, blogging/social media conferences, and homeschool conventions.

To inquire about availability, use the contact information below:

Email: michelle@withthehuddlestons.com

Facebook: www.facebook.com/withthehuddlestons

Website: withthehuddlestons.com/contact-us

When sending an email or private message, please include your name (first and last), email address, subject (book Michelle), and a detailed message explaining your inquiry. You will be contacted within 24 hours of your message being received.

Made in the USA
Lexington, KY
11 November 2018